Yuca Cookbook

Exploring the Versatile World of Yuca in 20 Delectable Recipes

YUCA COOKBOOK

First edition. January 25, 2024.

ISBN: 979-8224336203

Written by Sammy Andrews.

Table of Contents

Sammy Andrews

Chapter 1: Introduction to Yuca

What is Yuca?

Yuca, also known as cassava, manioc, or tapioca, is a starchy root vegetable that has been a dietary staple in many cultures around the world for centuries. This versatile tuber is native to South America and is a significant source of carbohydrates in many tropical regions. Its scientific name is Manihot esculenta.

Yuca has a tapered shape with rough, brown skin and a white or creamy interior flesh. It is a vital source of nutrition and sustenance for millions of people in Africa, Asia, the Americas, and the Caribbean. The root's popularity is due to its adaptability to various climates and its resistance to drought, making it a reliable crop even in challenging conditions.

History and Cultural Significance

Yuca in South America

Yuca has a rich history in South America, where it was first domesticated over 10,000 years ago by indigenous peoples in what is now Brazil. These early cultivators developed different varieties of yuca to suit their needs, such as sweet and bitter types. The sweet variety is what we commonly consume today, while the bitter type requires special processing to remove toxins.

In South America, yuca has been a dietary cornerstone for various indigenous groups, including the Arawak, Carib, and Taino peoples. It played a vital role in their daily sustenance and cultural rituals.

Yuca's Global Journey

Christopher Columbus is credited with introducing yuca to Europe after his voyages to the Americas in the late 15th century. From there, yuca rapidly spread across the globe, making its way to Africa, Asia, and other parts of the world. Yuca's adaptability to different climates and its high yield made it a valuable crop for food security.

In Africa, yuca became a crucial part of the diet, especially in countries like Nigeria, Ghana, and the Democratic Republic of Congo. It was integrated into traditional dishes and contributed to the rich culinary tapestry of the continent.

Nutritional Benefits

Yuca is not only a dietary staple but also a nutritious source of sustenance. Here are some of its nutritional benefits:

Carbohydrates: Yuca is rich in carbohydrates, making it an excellent energy source. It's a staple food in many regions where people engage in physically demanding activities.

Vitamins: Yuca contains essential vitamins such as vitamin C and B-complex vitamins. These vitamins support immune function and overall health.

Minerals: It provides minerals like potassium and magnesium, which are vital for heart health and muscle function.

Dietary Fiber: Yuca contains dietary fiber, aiding in digestion and promoting a feeling of fullness.

Low in Fat: Yuca is naturally low in fat, making it a healthy choice for those watching their fat intake.

Gluten-Free: Yuca is naturally gluten-free, making it suitable for those with gluten sensitivities or celiac disease.

In this cookbook, we will explore the culinary versatility of yuca, from traditional dishes to modern fusion creations. Get ready to embark on a flavorful journey through the world of yuca, where this humble root takes center stage in a variety of delicious recipes.

Chapter 2: Selecting and Preparing Yuca

Yuca, with its rich history and culinary diversity, can be a fantastic addition to your kitchen. But before you dive into creating delicious yuca dishes, it's essential to understand how to select, store, and prepare this versatile root vegetable.

How to Choose the Best Yuca

Selecting high-quality yuca is the first step towards a successful culinary experience. Here's how to choose the best yuca when shopping:

1. Appearance:

Look for yuca roots that are firm, straight, and well-shaped. Avoid those with wrinkles, soft spots, or any signs of mold or decay.

The skin should be smooth, tight, and free from blemishes. Some variation in skin color is normal, but avoid yucas with excessive dark spots or discoloration.

2. Size:

While there's no standard size for yuca, choose roots that are medium-sized. They are usually easier to work with and tend to have a better texture and flavor.

3. Texture:

Gently squeeze the yuca root. It should feel hard and dense, indicating freshness. If it feels spongy or has a hollow sound when tapped, it may be overripe.

4. Color:

The flesh of the yuca should be a creamy white or pale yellow color. Avoid any yuca with brown or grayish spots inside.

Proper Storage

Yuca can stay fresh for several weeks if stored correctly. Follow these guidelines to ensure your yuca remains in top condition:

1. Room Temperature:

Keep yuca at room temperature in a cool, dry place, similar to how you would store potatoes. It can be stored on the countertop or in a pantry.

2. Avoid Refrigeration:

Unlike many other vegetables, yuca should not be stored in the refrigerator. Cold temperatures can cause it to develop a hard, woody texture and lose flavor.

3. Ventilation:

Ensure proper ventilation to prevent moisture buildup, which can lead to mold. Store yuca in a well-ventilated area.

4. Separate from Other Produce:

Store yuca away from other fruits and vegetables, as some produce can emit ethylene gas, which may accelerate yuca ripening.

Peeling and Cutting Techniques

Preparing yuca for cooking involves peeling and sometimes cutting it into the desired shape. Follow these steps to peel and cut yuca effectively:

1. Wash and Scrub:

Before peeling, wash the yuca thoroughly under running water to remove any dirt or debris. Use a vegetable brush to scrub the skin clean.

2. Cut the Ends:

Using a sharp knife, cut off both ends of the yuca root.

3. Score the Skin:

Make a shallow, lengthwise cut along the yuca root's entire length, deep enough to penetrate the skin without cutting into the flesh.

4. Peel the Skin:

Use your fingers or a knife to gently pry off the skin in sections. Yuca skin can be tough, so take your time and be careful.

5. Remove the Inner Vein:

After peeling, you may notice a thin, woody core running through the center of the yuca. Remove it with a knife by making a lengthwise cut along the core and pulling it out.

6. Cut into Desired Shapes:

Now, you can cut the yuca into the desired shape for your recipe. Common options include cubes, strips, or rounds.

With these essential skills under your belt, you're ready to explore the world of yuca cuisine. In the upcoming chapters, we'll dive into a variety of yuca dishes, from classic recipes to innovative creations that showcase the incredible versatility of this root vegetable.

Chapter 3: Classic Yuca Dishes

In this chapter, we'll explore some classic yuca dishes that have been enjoyed for generations in various parts of the world. These recipes showcase the delicious simplicity of yuca and highlight its unique flavors and textures.

Yuca Fries with Garlic Aioli

Ingredients:

- 2 large yuca roots, peeled and cut into fries
- Vegetable oil for frying
- Salt and pepper to taste

For the Garlic Aioli:

- 1/2 cup mayonnaise
- 2 cloves garlic, minced
- 1 tablespoon lemon juice
- Salt and pepper to taste

Instructions:

Prepare the Yuca:

- Peel the yuca roots and cut them into fry-sized pieces, about 3-4 inches long and 1/2 inch wide.

Boil the Yuca:

- Place the yuca fries in a pot of boiling salted water. Cook for 10-15 minutes or until they are fork-tender but not mushy.

Drain and Dry:

- Drain the boiled yuca fries and pat them dry with a paper towel. Allow them to cool slightly.

Fry the Yuca:

- Heat vegetable oil in a deep fryer or large, heavy pot to 350°F (175°C).
- Carefully add the yuca fries to the hot oil in batches, frying until they are golden brown and crispy, about 3-4 minutes per batch.
- Remove with a slotted spoon and drain on paper towels.
- Season immediately with salt and pepper while they're still hot.

Prepare the Garlic Aioli:

- In a small bowl, combine mayonnaise, minced garlic, lemon juice, salt, and pepper. Mix well.

Serve:

- Serve the yuca fries hot with a side of garlic aioli for dipping. Enjoy!

Yuca con Mojo (Yuca with Garlic Sauce)
Ingredients:

- 2 large yuca roots, peeled and cut into chunks
- Salt for boiling

For the Mojo Sauce:

- 6 cloves garlic, minced
- 1/2 cup fresh lime juice
- 1/2 cup fresh orange juice

- 1/4 cup extra-virgin olive oil
- Salt and pepper to taste
- Fresh cilantro or parsley for garnish (optional)

Instructions:
Boil the Yuca:

- Place the yuca chunks in a large pot of salted boiling water. Cook for 15-20 minutes or until they are fork-tender.

Prepare the Mojo Sauce:

- While the yuca is boiling, prepare the mojo sauce. In a small saucepan, heat the olive oil over medium heat. Add the minced garlic and sauté for 1-2 minutes until fragrant, but do not let it brown.

- Add the lime juice and orange juice to the garlic and oil mixture. Simmer for a few minutes until the sauce thickens slightly. Season with salt and pepper to taste.

Drain and Serve:

- Drain the cooked yuca and transfer it to a serving platter.
- Pour the mojo sauce over the yuca.
- Garnish with fresh cilantro or parsley, if desired.

Serve:

- Serve the yuca con mojo as a flavorful side dish or a light appetizer. It's traditionally served warm, and the tangy garlic sauce perfectly complements the yuca's mild flavor.

Yuca and Cheese Empanadas
Ingredients:

- 2 cups mashed yuca (cooked and mashed yuca with a little butter and milk)
- 1 cup shredded mozzarella cheese
- 1/2 cup grated Parmesan cheese
- 1/2 teaspoon salt
- 1/4 teaspoon black pepper
- 1/2 teaspoon paprika
- 1 egg, beaten (for egg wash)
- Empanada dough (store-bought or homemade)

Instructions:
Prepare the Yuca Filling:

- In a mixing bowl, combine the mashed yuca, shredded mozzarella cheese, grated Parmesan cheese, salt, black pepper, and paprika. Mix well until all ingredients are evenly incorporated.

Assemble the Empanadas:

- Roll out the empanada dough and cut it into circles using a round cutter.
- Place a spoonful of the yuca and cheese mixture in the center of each dough circle.
- Fold the dough in half to create a semicircular shape, enclosing the filling.
- Use a fork to crimp the edges and seal the empanadas.

Bake or Fry:

- Preheat the oven to 375°F (190°C) if baking. Alternatively, you can deep-fry the empanadas.

- If baking, place the empanadas on a baking sheet lined with parchment paper. Brush the tops with beaten egg for a golden finish.
- Bake for 20-25 minutes or until the empanadas are golden brown and crispy.
- If frying, heat vegetable oil in a deep fryer or large, heavy pot to 350°F (175°C). Fry the empanadas until they are golden brown, about 3-4 minutes per batch. Drain on paper towels.

Serve:

- Serve the yuca and cheese empanadas hot as a delightful snack or appetizer. They're perfect for dipping in a zesty salsa or sauce of your choice.

These classic yuca dishes are a delightful introduction to the world of yuca cuisine. Each recipe offers a unique blend of flavors and textures, making them perfect for sharing with family and friends.

Chapter 4: Yuca Soups and Stews

In this chapter, we will explore the comforting and hearty world of yuca soups and stews. Yuca's starchy goodness lends itself beautifully to these dishes, creating a satisfying and flavorful experience.

Sancocho de Yuca (Yuca and Meat Stew)

Ingredients:

- 1 lb (450g) yuca, peeled and cut into chunks
- 1 lb (450g) bone-in chicken pieces (such as thighs or drumsticks)
- 1 lb (450g) beef stew meat, cubed
- 1 lb (450g) pork shoulder, cubed
- 1 large onion, chopped
- 4 cloves garlic, minced
- 1 bell pepper, chopped
- 2 tomatoes, chopped
- 2 carrots, peeled and sliced
- 2 corn cobs, cut into rounds
- 1 ripe plantain, peeled and sliced
- 1 teaspoon cumin
- 1 teaspoon oregano
- Salt and pepper to taste
- Water
- Fresh cilantro for garnish (optional)

Instructions:

Prepare the Meats:

- In a large pot, heat some oil over medium-high heat. Add the chicken, beef, and pork pieces, and brown them on all sides.

Remove and set aside.

Sauté Aromatics:

- In the same pot, add a bit more oil if needed. Sauté the onions, garlic, and bell pepper until they become fragrant and slightly softened.

Return Meats to Pot:

- Return the browned meats to the pot with the sautéed aromatics.

Add Vegetables and Spices:

- Add the chopped tomatoes, carrots, corn rounds, and plantain slices to the pot.
- Season with cumin, oregano, salt, and pepper.

Cover with Water:

- Pour enough water into the pot to cover all the ingredients. Bring it to a boil.

Simmer:

- Reduce the heat to low, cover, and simmer for about 30-40 minutes, or until the meats are tender and the yuca is cooked through.

Add Yuca:

- Add the yuca chunks to the pot and continue to simmer for an additional 15-20 minutes, or until the yuca is soft and easily pierced with a fork.

Serve:

- Ladle the sancocho into bowls, making sure to include a variety of meats, vegetables, and yuca chunks in each serving.
- Garnish with fresh cilantro, if desired.
- Serve hot and enjoy this hearty yuca and meat stew!

Yuca and Black Bean Soup
Ingredients:

- 1 lb (450g) yuca, peeled and diced
- 1 can (15 oz) black beans, drained and rinsed
- 1 onion, chopped
- 2 cloves garlic, minced
- 1 red bell pepper, chopped
- 1 teaspoon ground cumin
- 1 teaspoon chili powder
- 4 cups vegetable or chicken broth
- Salt and pepper to taste
- 2 tablespoons olive oil
- Sour cream and chopped fresh cilantro for garnish (optional)

Instructions:
Sauté Aromatics:

- In a large soup pot, heat the olive oil over medium heat. Add the chopped onion, garlic, and red bell pepper. Sauté until the vegetables are softened and fragrant.

Add Spices and Yuca:

- Stir in the ground cumin and chili powder. Add the diced yuca and cook for a few minutes, allowing the flavors to meld.

Pour in Broth:

- Pour in the vegetable or chicken broth, and bring the mixture to a boil.

Simmer:

- Reduce the heat to low, cover the pot, and let it simmer for about 20-25 minutes, or until the yuca is tender.

Blend or Mash:

- Use an immersion blender to partially blend the soup, leaving some chunks for texture. Alternatively, remove a portion of the soup and blend it in a regular blender before returning it to the pot.

Add Black Beans:

- Stir in the drained and rinsed black beans and cook for an additional 5-7 minutes, allowing them to heat through.

Season and Serve:

- Season the soup with salt and pepper to taste.
- Ladle the yuca and black bean soup into bowls and garnish with a dollop of sour cream and chopped fresh cilantro, if desired.

Creamy Yuca and Chicken Soup
Ingredients:

- 1 lb (450g) yuca, peeled and diced
- 1 lb (450g) boneless, skinless chicken breasts, cut into bite-sized pieces
- 1 onion, chopped
- 2 cloves garlic, minced
- 2 carrots, peeled and diced
- 2 celery stalks, diced
- 4 cups chicken broth
- 1 cup coconut milk
- 1 teaspoon curry powder

- 1/2 teaspoon turmeric
- Salt and pepper to taste
- Chopped fresh cilantro for garnish (optional)

Instructions:

Sauté Aromatics:

In a large soup pot, heat some oil over medium heat. Add the chopped onion, garlic, carrots, and celery. Sauté until the vegetables are softened and fragrant.

Add Chicken:

Add the diced chicken pieces to the pot and cook until they are no longer pink.

Add Spices and Yuca:

Stir in the curry powder and turmeric. Add the diced yuca and cook for a few minutes, allowing the flavors to meld.

Pour in Broth:

Pour in the chicken broth and bring the mixture to a boil.

Simmer:

Reduce the heat to low, cover the pot, and let it simmer for about 20-25 minutes, or until the yuca is tender and the chicken is cooked through.

Add Coconut Milk:

Stir in the coconut milk and heat the soup for an additional 5 minutes, making sure it's well combined.

Season and Serve:

- Season the creamy yuca and chicken soup with salt and pepper to taste.
- Ladle the soup into bowls and garnish with chopped fresh cilantro, if desired.

These yuca soups and stews offer warmth and comfort, making them perfect for a cozy meal, especially during cooler weather. Whether you prefer the richness of a stew or the creaminess of a soup, yuca adds a delightful twist to these classic dishes.

Chapter 5: Yuca Appetizers and Snacks

This chapter is dedicated to exploring the delightful world of yuca appetizers and snacks. From crispy croquettes to savory bites, these recipes are perfect for parties, gatherings, or simply satisfying your snack cravings.

Yuca Croquettes

Ingredients:

- 2 cups mashed yuca (cooked and mashed yuca with a little butter and milk)
- 1 cup cooked and shredded chicken or beef
- 1/2 cup finely chopped onion
- 1/4 cup finely chopped bell pepper (red or green)
- 2 cloves garlic, minced
- 1/4 cup chopped fresh cilantro
- 1/2 teaspoon cumin
- Salt and pepper to taste
- 1 cup breadcrumbs
- 2 eggs, beaten
- Vegetable oil for frying

Instructions:

Prepare the Filling:

- In a skillet, heat some oil over medium heat. Add the chopped onion, bell pepper, and minced garlic. Sauté until they are softened and fragrant.
- Add the shredded chicken or beef, cumin, salt, pepper, and chopped cilantro. Cook for a few minutes until everything is well combined and heated through. Remove from heat.

Assemble the Croquettes:

- Take a spoonful of the mashed yuca and flatten it in your hand.
- Place a spoonful of the meat filling in the center and fold the yuca over to encase the filling, forming a croquette shape.
- Repeat this process with the remaining yuca and filling.

Coat in Breadcrumbs:

- Dip each croquette into beaten egg and then coat it in breadcrumbs, ensuring an even coating.

Fry the Croquettes:

- Heat vegetable oil in a deep fryer or large, heavy pot to 350°F (175°C).
- Carefully add the yuca croquettes to the hot oil and fry until they are golden brown and crispy, about 3-4 minutes per batch.
- Remove with a slotted spoon and drain on paper towels.

Serve:

- Serve the yuca croquettes hot as a delicious appetizer or snack. They pair perfectly with a dipping sauce of your choice.

Yuca Chips with Salsa Verde
Ingredients:

- 2 cups yuca, peeled and thinly sliced into rounds
- Vegetable oil for frying
- Salt to taste
- 1 cup salsa verde (store-bought or homemade)

Instructions:
Prepare the Yuca Chips:

- Heat vegetable oil in a deep fryer or large, heavy pot to 350°F (175°C).
- Carefully add the thinly sliced yuca rounds to the hot oil, working in batches to avoid overcrowding.
- Fry until the yuca slices are golden brown and crispy, about 2-3 minutes per batch.
- Remove with a slotted spoon and drain on paper towels.
- Sprinkle with salt while they're still hot.

Serve with Salsa Verde:

Arrange the yuca chips on a serving platter and serve them with a side of salsa verde for dipping. The tangy salsa complements the crunchy yuca chips beautifully.

Yuca and Chorizo Bites

Ingredients:

- 2 cups mashed yuca (cooked and mashed yuca with a little butter and milk)
- 1/2 cup cooked and crumbled chorizo sausage
- 1/4 cup grated cheddar cheese
- 1/4 cup chopped fresh cilantro
- Salt and pepper to taste
- 1 cup panko breadcrumbs
- 2 eggs, beaten
- Vegetable oil for frying

Instructions:

Prepare the Filling:

In a mixing bowl, combine the mashed yuca, crumbled chorizo sausage, grated cheddar cheese, chopped cilantro, salt, and pepper. Mix well until all ingredients are evenly incorporated.

Shape into Bites:

Take a small portion of the yuca mixture and shape it into a bite-sized ball or cylinder. Repeat this process with the remaining mixture.

Coat in Breadcrumbs:

Dip each yuca and chorizo bite into beaten egg and then coat it in panko breadcrumbs, ensuring an even coating.

Fry the Bites:

- Heat vegetable oil in a deep fryer or large, heavy pot to 350°F (175°C).
- Carefully add the yuca and chorizo bites to the hot oil and fry until they are golden brown and crispy, about 3-4 minutes per batch.
- Remove with a slotted spoon and drain on paper towels.

Serve:

Serve the yuca and chorizo bites hot as a flavorful appetizer or snack. They're perfect for dipping in salsa or a zesty aioli.

These yuca appetizers and snacks offer a variety of flavors and textures, making them ideal for entertaining or simply enjoying a tasty bite. Feel free to get creative with your choice of dips and sauces to customize your snacking experience.

Chapter 6: Yuca in Main Courses

In this chapter, we'll explore how yuca can take center stage in main course dishes. From a classic Cuban dish to innovative creations, these recipes showcase the versatility and deliciousness of yuca in main courses.

Ropa Vieja with Yuca Mash

Ingredients:

- 2 lbs (900g) flank steak
- 1 onion, chopped
- 1 bell pepper, chopped
- 3 cloves garlic, minced
- 1 can (14 oz) crushed tomatoes
- 1/2 cup beef broth
- 1 teaspoon ground cumin
- 1 teaspoon smoked paprika
- Salt and pepper to taste
- 2 bay leaves
- Vegetable oil for searing
- Fresh cilantro or parsley for garnish
- Yuca mash (see Chapter 2)

Instructions:

Sear the Flank Steak:

Season the flank steak with salt and pepper. In a large skillet or Dutch oven, heat vegetable oil over high heat. Sear the steak on both sides until well-browned. Remove and set aside.

Sauté Aromatics:

In the same skillet, add a bit more oil if needed. Sauté the chopped onion, bell pepper, and minced garlic until they become fragrant and slightly softened.

Simmer the Ropa Vieja:

Return the seared flank steak to the skillet. Add crushed tomatoes, beef broth, ground cumin, smoked paprika, bay leaves, and additional salt and pepper if needed.

Cover and simmer on low heat for 2-3 hours or until the meat is tender and can be easily shredded with a fork.

Shred the Meat:

Remove the cooked flank steak from the skillet and shred it using two forks. Return the shredded meat to the skillet and simmer for an additional 15-20 minutes, allowing it to absorb the flavors.

Serve with Yuca Mash:

Serve the Ropa Vieja hot over a bed of yuca mash. Garnish with fresh cilantro or parsley for added flavor and color.

Yuca-Crusted Fish Fillets

Ingredients:

- 4 fish fillets (such as tilapia, cod, or snapper)
- 2 cups mashed yuca (cooked and mashed yuca with a little butter and milk)
- 1/2 cup breadcrumbs
- 1/4 cup grated Parmesan cheese
- 1 teaspoon dried oregano
- 1/2 teaspoon garlic powder
- Salt and pepper to taste
- Olive oil for brushing
- Lemon wedges for serving

Instructions:

Prepare the Yuca Crust:

In a mixing bowl, combine the mashed yuca, breadcrumbs, grated Parmesan cheese, dried oregano, garlic powder, salt, and pepper. Mix until you have a crumbly mixture.

Coat the Fish Fillets:

- Brush the fish fillets with a bit of olive oil on both sides.
- Press the yuca crust mixture onto both sides of each fish fillet, ensuring an even coating.

Bake the Fish:

- Preheat the oven to 375°F (190°C). Place the coated fish fillets on a baking sheet lined with parchment paper.
- Bake for 15-20 minutes or until the fish is cooked through and the yuca crust is golden brown and crispy.

Serve:

Serve the yuca-crusted fish fillets hot with lemon wedges on the side for a zesty kick.

Yuca Gnocchi with Pesto
Ingredients:

- 2 cups mashed yuca (cooked and mashed yuca with a little butter and milk)
- 1 cup all-purpose flour, plus extra for dusting
- 1 egg
- Salt and pepper to taste
- Pesto sauce (store-bought or homemade)
- Grated Parmesan cheese for garnish
- Fresh basil leaves for garnish

Instructions:
Prepare the Yuca Gnocchi Dough:
In a mixing bowl, combine the mashed yuca, all-purpose flour, egg, salt, and pepper. Mix until you have a smooth, pliable dough. If the dough is too sticky, add a bit more flour as needed.

Form the Gnocchi:
On a lightly floured surface, roll the yuca dough into a long rope, about 1-inch thick. Cut the rope into bite-sized pieces, shaping each piece into a small gnocchi by rolling it gently with the tines of a fork or your fingers.

Boil the Gnocchi:
Bring a large pot of salted water to a boil. Carefully add the yuca gnocchi to the boiling water. They will float to the surface when they are cooked, which usually takes about 2-3 minutes. Remove them with a slotted spoon and set aside.

Toss with Pesto:
In a serving bowl, toss the cooked yuca gnocchi with your favorite pesto sauce until well coated.

Serve:

Serve the yuca gnocchi with pesto hot, garnished with grated Parmesan cheese and fresh basil leaves.

These main course dishes highlight yuca's ability to transform into a satisfying and flavorful centerpiece. Whether you're in the mood for a rich Cuban classic or a unique yuca-crusted fish fillet, these recipes offer delicious options for your dinner table.

Chapter 7: Yuca in International Cuisine

Yuca's versatility shines when it's used in international dishes that span the globe. From African and Caribbean influences to Brazilian delicacies and Latin-inspired creations, these recipes celebrate the rich diversity of yuca in global cuisine.

Yuca Fufu (African and Caribbean Influence)
Ingredients:

- 2 cups peeled and cubed yuca
- 2 cups water
- Salt to taste
- 2 tablespoons butter
- Optional toppings: sautéed vegetables, stewed meats, or a savory sauce

Instructions:
Prepare the Yuca:

- In a large pot, bring 2 cups of water to a boil. Add a pinch of salt.
- Add the peeled and cubed yuca to the boiling water. Cook for 20-25 minutes or until the yuca is fork-tender and can be easily mashed.

Mash the Yuca:

- Drain the cooked yuca and transfer it to a mixing bowl. Add the butter and a pinch of salt.
- Mash the yuca until it becomes smooth and pliable. You can use a potato masher or your hands to achieve the desired

consistency.

Shape into Fufu Balls:

Wet your hands and shape the mashed yuca into small round balls or discs.

Serve with Toppings:

Yuca fufu is traditionally served with sautéed vegetables, stewed meats, or a flavorful sauce of your choice. Create your own fufu bowl with your favorite toppings.

Brazilian Yuca Balls (Bolinhos de Mandioca)
Ingredients:

- 2 cups mashed yuca (cooked and mashed yuca with a little butter and milk)
- 1/2 cup cooked and crumbled chorizo sausage
- 1/4 cup finely chopped red bell pepper
- 1/4 cup finely chopped onion
- 1/4 cup grated Parmesan cheese
- Salt and pepper to taste
- Vegetable oil for frying
- Lime wedges for serving

Instructions:
Prepare the Yuca Balls:

In a mixing bowl, combine the mashed yuca, crumbled chorizo sausage, chopped red bell pepper, chopped onion, grated Parmesan cheese, salt, and pepper. Mix until all ingredients are well incorporated.

Shape into Balls:

Take a small portion of the yuca mixture and shape it into small balls.

Fry the Bolinhos:

- Heat vegetable oil in a deep fryer or large, heavy pot to 350°F (175°C).
- Carefully add the yuca balls to the hot oil and fry until they are golden brown and crispy, about 3-4 minutes per batch.
- Remove with a slotted spoon and drain on paper towels.

Serve with Lime Wedges:

Serve the Brazilian yuca balls hot with lime wedges on the side for a zesty kick.

Yuca Tacos with Latin Flavors
Ingredients:

- 1 lb (450g) yuca, peeled and cut into thin strips
- Vegetable oil for frying
- Salt and pepper to taste
- 8 small corn or flour tortillas
- 1 cup shredded cabbage
- 1 cup diced tomatoes
- 1 cup diced red onion
- 1 cup chopped fresh cilantro
- 1 cup crumbled queso fresco or feta cheese
- Lime wedges for serving
- Hot sauce or salsa of your choice

Instructions:
Prepare the Yuca Strips:

- Heat vegetable oil in a deep fryer or large, heavy pot to 350°F (175°C).
- Carefully add the yuca strips to the hot oil and fry until they are golden brown and crispy, about 3-4 minutes. Remove with a slotted spoon and drain on paper towels.
- Season with salt and pepper while they're still hot.

Assemble the Tacos:

- Warm the tortillas in a dry skillet or microwave.
- Fill each tortilla with a portion of fried yuca strips, shredded cabbage, diced tomatoes, diced red onion, chopped cilantro, and crumbled queso fresco or feta cheese.

Serve with Lime Wedges and Sauce:

Serve the yuca tacos hot, garnished with lime wedges and your choice of hot sauce or salsa. Squeeze lime juice over the tacos before eating for added flavor.

These international yuca recipes offer a taste of different cultures and regions, showcasing the versatility of this root vegetable in various culinary traditions. Whether you're craving the comforting flavors of yuca fufu, the boldness of Brazilian bolinhos, or the zesty freshness of yuca tacos, these dishes are sure to satisfy your taste buds.

Chapter 8: Vegan and Vegetarian Yuca Creations

For those following vegan or vegetarian diets, yuca offers a wonderful canvas for creating flavorful and satisfying dishes. In this chapter, we'll explore a variety of plant-based yuca creations that are both delicious and nutritious.

Vegan Yuca Ceviche

Ingredients:

- 2 cups peeled and cubed yuca
- 1 cup diced red onion
- 1 cup diced tomatoes
- 1 cup diced cucumber
- 1/2 cup diced red bell pepper
- 1/4 cup chopped fresh cilantro
- Juice of 3-4 limes
- 2 tablespoons olive oil
- 1 jalapeño pepper, finely chopped (optional for heat)
- Salt and pepper to taste
- Avocado slices for garnish (optional)

Instructions:

Prepare the Yuca:

- In a large pot, bring water to a boil. Add a pinch of salt and the peeled and cubed yuca. Cook for 20-25 minutes or until the yuca is fork-tender but not mushy. Drain and set aside to cool.

Marinate the Yuca:

- In a large mixing bowl, combine the cooked yuca cubes with diced red onion, diced tomatoes, diced cucumber, diced red bell

pepper, and chopped cilantro.
- In a separate bowl, whisk together the lime juice, olive oil, jalapeño (if using), salt, and pepper. Pour this dressing over the yuca and vegetables. Toss gently to combine.

Chill and Serve:

- Cover the bowl and refrigerate the vegan yuca ceviche for at least 30 minutes to allow the flavors to meld.
- Serve chilled, garnished with avocado slices if desired.

Yuca and Black Bean Tacos (Vegan)
Ingredients:

- 2 cups peeled and cubed yuca
- 1 can (15 oz) black beans, drained and rinsed
- 1 cup diced tomatoes
- 1 cup diced red onion
- 1/2 cup chopped fresh cilantro
- 1 tablespoon olive oil
- 1 teaspoon ground cumin
- 1/2 teaspoon chili powder
- Salt and pepper to taste
- 8 small corn or flour tortillas
- Lime wedges for serving
- Guacamole or salsa for topping (optional)

Instructions:

Prepare the Yuca:

In a large pot, bring water to a boil. Add a pinch of salt and the peeled and cubed yuca. Cook for 20-25 minutes or until the yuca is fork-tender. Drain and set aside.

Prepare the Filling:

- In a skillet, heat olive oil over medium heat. Add diced red onion and sauté until it becomes translucent and slightly softened.
- Add diced tomatoes, black beans, ground cumin, chili powder, salt, and pepper. Cook for 5-7 minutes, allowing the flavors to meld.

Mash and Mix:

- In a mixing bowl, mash the cooked yuca until it's smooth and pliable.

- Add the black bean and tomato mixture to the mashed yuca. Stir in chopped cilantro and mix until well combined.

Assemble the Tacos:

- Warm the tortillas in a dry skillet or microwave.
- Fill each tortilla with a portion of the yuca and black bean mixture.

Serve with Lime Wedges:

- Serve the vegan yuca and black bean tacos hot, with lime wedges on the side. Add guacamole or salsa if desired.

Yuca and Mushroom Stir-Fry (Vegetarian)
Ingredients:

- 2 cups peeled and cubed yuca
- 2 cups sliced mushrooms (your choice of variety)
- 1 cup sliced bell peppers (assorted colors)
- 1 cup sliced red onion
- 2 cloves garlic, minced
- 1/4 cup soy sauce or tamari (for a gluten-free option)
- 2 tablespoons vegetable oil
- 1 teaspoon sesame oil (optional)
- 1 teaspoon ginger, minced
- 1 teaspoon cornstarch mixed with 2 tablespoons water
- Fresh cilantro or green onions for garnish
- Cooked rice or noodles for serving (optional)

Instructions:
Prepare the Yuca:
In a large pot, bring water to a boil. Add a pinch of salt and the peeled and cubed yuca. Cook for 20-25 minutes or until the yuca is fork-tender but not mushy. Drain and set aside.

Stir-Fry the Vegetables:

In a large skillet or wok, heat vegetable oil over high heat. Add minced garlic and sliced red onion. Stir-fry for 1-2 minutes until fragrant.

Add Mushrooms and Bell Peppers:

Add sliced mushrooms and bell peppers to the skillet. Stir-fry for 3-5 minutes until they begin to soften and the mushrooms release their moisture.

Add Yuca and Sauce:

- Add the cooked yuca cubes to the skillet.
- In a small bowl, mix soy sauce (or tamari), sesame oil (if using), minced ginger, and the cornstarch-water mixture. Pour this sauce over the stir-fry.

Toss and Serve:

Stir-fry everything together for an additional 2-3 minutes until the sauce thickens and coats the ingredients.

Garnish and Serve:

- Garnish the yuca and mushroom stir-fry with fresh cilantro or green onions.
- Serve hot on its own or over cooked rice or noodles, if desired.

These vegan and vegetarian yuca creations are not only packed with flavor but also showcase the plant-based potential of yuca in your meals. Whether you're enjoying a refreshing yuca ceviche, hearty yuca and black bean tacos, or a savory yuca and mushroom stir-fry, these dishes are perfect for those seeking meat-free options.

Chapter 9: Gluten-Free Yuca Delights

For those who follow a gluten-free diet, yuca is a wonderful alternative to traditional wheat-based flours. In this chapter, we'll explore a range of gluten-free yuca creations that are both delicious and accommodating to dietary restrictions.

Yuca Flour in Baking

Introduction:

Yuca flour, also known as cassava flour, is a versatile gluten-free flour that can be used in various baking recipes. It offers a unique texture and flavor to your favorite baked goods while keeping them gluten-free. Below, you'll find a basic recipe for yuca flour and some ideas for using it in your baking endeavors.

Basic Yuca Flour Recipe:

Ingredients:

- 1 lb (450g) yuca root, peeled and chopped

Instructions:

Peel and Chop the Yuca:

Start by peeling the yuca root and chopping it into small pieces.

Boil the Yuca:

- Place the chopped yuca in a large pot and cover it with water. Add a pinch of salt.
- Bring the water to a boil and simmer for about 20-25 minutes or until the yuca is fork-tender.

Drain and Mash:

- Drain the boiled yuca and transfer it to a mixing bowl.
- Mash the yuca until it forms a smooth, dough-like consistency.

Dry and Grind:

- Spread the mashed yuca onto a baking sheet and allow it to cool completely.
- Once cooled, grind the yuca into a fine powder using a food processor or blender. This is your homemade yuca flour.

Ideas for Using Yuca Flour in Baking:

- Substitute yuca flour for regular wheat flour in your favorite cookie, cake, or muffin recipes.
- Use yuca flour as a thickening agent in gluten-free sauces and gravies.
- Create gluten-free pancakes and waffles using a blend of yuca flour and other gluten-free flours.
- Experiment with yuca flour in gluten-free bread recipes for a unique texture and flavor.

Yuca Pizza Crust
Ingredients:

- 2 cups yuca flour
- 1 teaspoon baking powder
- 1/2 teaspoon salt
- 2 tablespoons olive oil
- 2/3 cup warm water
- Pizza sauce
- Cheese and your favorite toppings

Instructions:
Prepare the Dough:

- In a mixing bowl, combine yuca flour, baking powder, and salt. Mix well.

- Add olive oil and warm water to the dry ingredients. Stir until a dough forms. Knead the dough for a few minutes until it's smooth and pliable.

Roll Out the Crust:

- Preheat your oven to 450°F (230°C). Place a piece of parchment paper on a baking sheet.
- Roll out the yuca pizza dough into a thin crust on the parchment paper.

Bake the Crust:

- Bake the crust in the preheated oven for about 10 minutes or until it's slightly golden.

Add Toppings:

- Remove the crust from the oven and spread pizza sauce, cheese, and your favorite toppings over it.

Bake Again:

- Return the pizza to the oven and bake for an additional 10-15 minutes or until the cheese is bubbly and golden.

Slice and Serve:

- Slice the yuca pizza into portions and serve hot.

Yuca Pancakes
Ingredients:

- 1 cup yuca flour
- 2 tablespoons sugar
- 1 teaspoon baking powder
- 1/4 teaspoon salt
- 1 cup almond milk (or any plant-based milk)
- 1 teaspoon vanilla extract
- 2 tablespoons vegetable oil
- Fresh fruit or maple syrup for topping (optional)

Instructions:
Prepare the Batter:
In a mixing bowl, combine yuca flour, sugar, baking powder, and salt. Mix well.
Add Wet Ingredients:
Add almond milk, vanilla extract, and vegetable oil to the dry ingredients. Stir until the batter is smooth.

Cook the Pancakes:

- Heat a non-stick skillet or griddle over medium-high heat and lightly grease it.
- Pour ladles of batter onto the hot skillet to form pancakes. Cook until bubbles form on the surface, then flip and cook the other side until golden brown.

Serve:

Serve the yuca pancakes hot, topped with fresh fruit or drizzled with maple syrup if desired.

These gluten-free yuca delights offer a tasty alternative for those with dietary restrictions while providing the unique flavors and textures that yuca brings to the table. Whether you're using yuca flour in baking, creating a gluten-free pizza crust, or whipping up a stack of yuca pancakes, you'll discover the endless possibilities of gluten-free cooking with yuca.

Chapter 10: Sweet Yuca Treats

Yuca is not just for savory dishes; it can also be used to create delicious sweet treats. In this chapter, we'll explore a selection of sweet yuca creations that will satisfy your sweet tooth and introduce you to the delightful world of yuca-based desserts.

Yuca and Coconut Cake

Ingredients:

- 2 cups peeled and cubed yuca
- 1 cup coconut milk
- 1 cup sugar
- 3 eggs
- 1/4 cup melted butter
- 1 teaspoon vanilla extract
- 1 cup shredded coconut (sweetened or unsweetened)
- 1/2 teaspoon baking powder
- Pinch of salt
- Powdered sugar for dusting (optional)

Instructions:

Prepare the Yuca:

In a large pot, bring water to a boil. Add a pinch of salt and the peeled and cubed yuca. Cook for 20-25 minutes or until the yuca is fork-tender. Drain and set aside.

Blend the Yuca:

In a blender or food processor, combine the cooked yuca, coconut milk, sugar, eggs, melted butter, and vanilla extract. Blend until you have a smooth mixture.

Combine Dry Ingredients:

In a mixing bowl, combine shredded coconut, baking powder, and a pinch of salt.

Mix Wet and Dry Ingredients:

Pour the blended yuca mixture into the bowl with the dry ingredients. Stir until well combined.

Bake the Cake:

- Preheat your oven to 350°F (175°C). Grease a baking dish or cake pan.
- Pour the cake batter into the prepared pan.
- Bake for approximately 30-35 minutes or until the cake is set and the top is golden brown.

Cool and Dust with Powdered Sugar:

- Allow the yuca and coconut cake to cool in the pan for a few minutes before transferring it to a wire rack to cool completely.
- Once cooled, you can dust the top with powdered sugar for a finishing touch.

Yuca Pudding with Caramel Sauce
Ingredients:

- 2 cups peeled and cubed yuca
- 1 cup coconut milk
- 1/2 cup sugar
- 1/4 teaspoon salt
- 1/2 teaspoon vanilla extract
- Caramel sauce (store-bought or homemade)

Instructions:
Prepare the Yuca:

In a large pot, bring water to a boil. Add a pinch of salt and the peeled and cubed yuca. Cook for 20-25 minutes or until the yuca is fork-tender. Drain and set aside.

Blend the Yuca:

In a blender or food processor, combine the cooked yuca, coconut milk, sugar, salt, and vanilla extract. Blend until you have a smooth and creamy mixture.

Serve with Caramel Sauce:

- Spoon the yuca pudding into individual serving dishes.
- Drizzle caramel sauce over the top of each serving.
- Serve warm or chilled, depending on your preference.

Yuca and Chocolate Brownies
Ingredients:

- 2 cups peeled and cubed yuca
- 1/2 cup cocoa powder
- 1/2 cup sugar
- 1/4 cup melted coconut oil
- 2 eggs
- 1 teaspoon vanilla extract
- 1/2 teaspoon baking powder
- 1/4 teaspoon salt
- 1/2 cup chocolate chips (optional)

Instructions:
Prepare the Yuca:

In a large pot, bring water to a boil. Add a pinch of salt and the peeled and cubed yuca. Cook for 20-25 minutes or until the yuca is fork-tender. Drain and set aside.

Blend the Yuca:

In a blender or food processor, combine the cooked yuca, cocoa powder, sugar, melted coconut oil, eggs, vanilla extract, baking powder, and a pinch of salt. Blend until you have a smooth and chocolatey batter.

Add Chocolate Chips (Optional):

If you desire extra chocolate goodness, fold in chocolate chips into the batter.

Bake the Brownies:

- Preheat your oven to 350°F (175°C). Grease a baking dish or brownie pan.
- Pour the brownie batter into the prepared pan and spread it evenly.
- Bake for approximately 20-25 minutes or until a toothpick inserted into the center comes out with a few moist crumbs.

Cool and Cut:

Allow the yuca and chocolate brownies to cool in the pan before cutting them into squares or rectangles.

These sweet yuca treats demonstrate the incredible versatility of yuca in the realm of desserts. Whether you're indulging in a moist yuca and coconut cake, savoring a creamy yuca pudding with caramel sauce, or enjoying the rich chocolatey goodness of yuca and chocolate brownies, these desserts are sure to delight your taste buds.

Chapter 11: Yuca Beverages

Yuca isn't just for solid dishes; it can also be incorporated into a variety of delightful beverages. In this chapter, we'll explore refreshing and unique yuca-based drinks that will quench your thirst and introduce you to the wonderful world of yuca beverages.

Yuca Smoothie

Ingredients:

- 1 cup peeled and cubed yuca
- 1 ripe banana
- 1/2 cup pineapple chunks (fresh or frozen)
- 1/2 cup mango chunks (fresh or frozen)
- 1/2 cup coconut milk
- 1/2 cup almond milk (or any preferred milk)
- 1 tablespoon honey or maple syrup (optional for sweetness)
- Ice cubes (optional)
- Fresh mint leaves for garnish (optional)

Instructions:

Prepare the Yuca:

In a large pot, bring water to a boil. Add a pinch of salt and the peeled and cubed yuca. Cook for 20-25 minutes or until the yuca is fork-tender. Drain and set aside to cool.

Blend the Ingredients:

- In a blender, combine the cooked yuca, ripe banana, pineapple chunks, mango chunks, coconut milk, almond milk, and honey or maple syrup (if using).
- If you prefer a colder smoothie, you can add a handful of ice cubes as well.

Blend Until Smooth:

Blend all the ingredients until you achieve a smooth and creamy consistency.

Serve:

- Pour the yuca smoothie into glasses.
- Garnish with fresh mint leaves if desired.
- Serve immediately and enjoy the tropical flavors!

Yuca Horchata
Ingredients:

- 1 cup peeled and cubed yuca
- 1 cup rice (white or brown)
- 4 cups water
- 1 cinnamon stick
- 1/2 cup sugar (adjust to taste)
- 1/2 teaspoon vanilla extract
- Ground cinnamon for garnish (optional)
- Ice cubes (optional)

Instructions:
Prepare the Yuca:
In a large pot, bring water to a boil. Add a pinch of salt and the peeled and cubed yuca. Cook for 20-25 minutes or until the yuca is fork-tender. Drain and set aside.
Prepare the Rice:

- In a separate pot, rinse the rice thoroughly.
- Add 4 cups of water and the cinnamon stick to the rice.
- Bring to a boil, then reduce the heat and simmer for about 20-25 minutes, or until the rice is fully cooked and the mixture thickens.

Blend Yuca and Rice:
In a blender, combine the cooked yuca and the cooked rice (with the cinnamon stick removed). Blend until you have a smooth mixture.
Sweeten and Flavor:
Add sugar and vanilla extract to the blender and blend again until the horchata is sweetened to your liking.
Chill and Serve:

- Transfer the yuca horchata to a pitcher and refrigerate until cold.

- Serve the horchata over ice cubes, garnished with a sprinkle of ground cinnamon if desired.

Yuca Mojito
Ingredients:

- 1 cup peeled and cubed yuca
- 1 lime, cut into wedges
- 1/4 cup fresh mint leaves
- 2 tablespoons sugar
- 2 ounces white rum (optional)
- Club soda
- Ice cubes

Instructions:
Prepare the Yuca:
In a large pot, bring water to a boil. Add a pinch of salt and the peeled and cubed yuca. Cook for 20-25 minutes or until the yuca is fork-tender. Drain and set aside to cool.
Muddle the Ingredients:
In a glass, muddle fresh mint leaves, sugar, and lime wedges together until the mint releases its fragrance.

Blend the Yuca:
In a blender, combine the cooked yuca with a bit of water. Blend until you have a smooth yuca puree.
Mix the Yuca and Mint:
Add the yuca puree to the glass with the muddled mint, sugar, and lime. Stir well to combine.
Add Rum (Optional) and Ice:

- If you desire an alcoholic version, add white rum to the glass and stir.
- Add ice cubes to the glass.

Top with Club Soda:
Fill the glass with club soda to your desired level, stirring gently.
Serve:

- Serve the yuca mojito cold and garnish with additional mint leaves and lime wedges if desired.

These yuca-based beverages offer a unique twist on classic drinks and provide a refreshing way to enjoy yuca in liquid form.

Chapter 12: Exploring Yuca Varieties

While yuca, also known as cassava, is primarily known for its starchy root, there are other parts and varieties of this versatile plant that can be used in culinary creations. In this chapter, we'll dive into different yuca varieties and explore their unique culinary uses.

Purple Yuca

Introduction:

Purple yuca is a vibrant and visually stunning variety of yuca known for its deep purple or violet-colored flesh. It offers a delightful twist on the traditional white yuca, not only in appearance but also in flavor. Here, we'll explore how to cook and enjoy purple yuca.

Cooking Purple Yuca:

Peel and Prepare:

Start by peeling the purple yuca, just like you would with white yuca. The vibrant purple color is hidden beneath the skin.

Boil or Steam:

Cook purple yuca by boiling or steaming it until it's fork-tender. This usually takes 20-25 minutes.

Serve:

Once cooked, you can use purple yuca in various recipes where you would use white yuca. The purple variety has a slightly nuttier and earthier flavor, making it a unique addition to your dishes.

Yuca Harina (Yuca Flour)

Introduction:

Yuca harina, also known as cassava flour or yuca starch, is a gluten-free flour made from the dried and ground roots of the yuca plant. It is widely used in many culinary applications and can be a great gluten-free alternative to wheat flour.

Uses of Yuca Harina:

Gluten-Free Baking:

Yuca harina can be used as a one-to-one substitute for wheat flour in gluten-free baking. It works well in recipes for bread, muffins, pancakes, and more.

Thickening Agent:

Yuca harina is an excellent thickening agent for soups, stews, sauces, and gravies. It imparts a neutral flavor while providing thickening power.

Breading and Coating:

Use yuca harina to bread and coat foods before frying or baking. It creates a crispy, golden crust.

Dumplings and Noodles:

Yuca harina can be used to make gluten-free dumplings and noodles. These can be added to soups or enjoyed as a side dish.

Yuca Leaves in Cooking

Introduction:

While yuca roots are the most commonly consumed part of the plant, yuca leaves also have culinary value in some cultures. They are known for their slightly bitter flavor and are often used in traditional dishes.

Cooking with Yuca Leaves:

Harvest and Prepare:

Yuca leaves are typically harvested from mature yuca plants. The leaves should be fresh and free of blemishes.

Boil and Cook:

Yuca leaves need to be boiled or cooked before consumption. Boil them until they are tender, which may take 15-20 minutes.

Flavorful Dishes:

Yuca leaves are commonly used in dishes like "Cassava Leaf Soup" in West African cuisine and "Ecuadorian Yuca with Peanut Sauce." They can also be added to stews for flavor.

Consideration:

Be aware that yuca leaves contain compounds called cyanogenic glycosides, which can be toxic if not properly prepared. Boiling or cooking the leaves effectively removes these toxins.

Exploring different yuca varieties and parts of the plant allows you to add diversity to your culinary repertoire. Whether you're experimenting with the unique flavors of purple yuca, incorporating gluten-free yuca harina into your baking, or exploring the culinary potential of yuca leaves, you'll discover the versatility of this remarkable plant.

Chapter 13: Fermented Yuca Recipes

Fermentation is a fascinating culinary technique that can enhance the flavor and nutritional value of various foods, including yuca. In this chapter, we'll explore how to ferment yuca and create delectable dishes that incorporate the unique tangy notes and probiotics that fermentation provides.

Yuca Arepas

Ingredients:

- 2 cups peeled and grated yuca
- 1/2 cup water
- 1/2 cup sourdough starter or kefir
- 1 teaspoon salt
- 1 tablespoon olive oil

Instructions:

Prepare the Yuca Dough:

In a mixing bowl, combine grated yuca, water, sourdough starter or kefir, and salt. Mix well until you have a dough-like consistency.

Shape the Arepas:

Divide the yuca dough into small portions and shape them into flat, round discs, similar to thick pancakes.

Cook the Arepas:

- Heat olive oil in a skillet over medium heat.
- Place the yuca arepas in the skillet and cook for 4-5 minutes on each side, or until they are golden brown and cooked through.

Serve:

Serve the yuca arepas warm, as a side dish or with your favorite toppings.

Yuca Bread
Ingredients:

- 2 cups peeled and grated yuca
- 1/2 cup water
- 1/2 cup sourdough starter
- 2 cups yuca harina (cassava flour)
- 1 teaspoon salt
- 1 tablespoon olive oil

Instructions:
Prepare the Yuca Dough:
In a mixing bowl, combine grated yuca, water, sourdough starter, yuca harina, and salt. Mix well until you have a dough.
Knead and Shape the Bread:

- Knead the dough for a few minutes until it becomes smooth and elastic.
- Shape the dough into a round loaf or place it in a greased loaf pan.

Let It Rise:

Cover the dough with a clean kitchen towel and let it rise for about 4-6 hours or until it has doubled in size. This slow fermentation process enhances the flavor.

Bake:

- Preheat your oven to 375°F (190°C).
- If you shaped the dough into a loaf, brush the top with olive oil.
- Bake in the preheated oven for 30-40 minutes or until the bread is golden brown and sounds hollow when tapped on the bottom.

Cool and Serve:

Allow the yuca bread to cool before slicing and serving. Enjoy it with your favorite spreads or toppings.

Yuca Sour Mash
Ingredients:

- 2 cups peeled and grated yuca
- 1/2 cup water
- 1/2 cup sourdough starter

Instructions:
Prepare the Mash:
In a clean glass jar, combine grated yuca, water, and sourdough starter. Stir well to thoroughly mix the ingredients.
Ferment:

- Cover the jar loosely with a lid or a clean cloth secured with a rubber band.
- Allow the yuca sour mash to ferment at room temperature for 24-48 hours. During this time, the mixture will develop a tangy and slightly sour flavor.

Store:
Once the sour mash has reached your desired level of sourness, seal the jar with an airtight lid and refrigerate it. It can be used as a flavor enhancer in various recipes.

These fermented yuca recipes offer a unique twist on traditional yuca dishes. Whether you're enjoying the tangy goodness of yuca arepas, savoring the hearty flavor of yuca bread, or experimenting with the probiotic-rich yuca sour mash, these recipes showcase the culinary possibilities that fermentation can bring to yuca-based cuisine.

Chapter 14: Preserving Yuca

Preserving yuca allows you to enjoy its delicious flavors and versatility year-round. In this chapter, we'll explore various methods for preserving yuca, from pickling to making jams and freeze-drying.

Yuca Pickles

Ingredients:

- 2 cups peeled and sliced yuca
- 1 cup white vinegar
- 1 cup water
- 1/4 cup sugar
- 1 tablespoon salt
- 2 cloves garlic, minced
- 1 teaspoon mustard seeds
- 1 teaspoon whole black peppercorns
- 1 bay leaf

Instructions:

Prepare the Yuca:

Peel and slice the yuca into thin rounds or strips.

Prepare the Brine:

In a saucepan, combine white vinegar, water, sugar, salt, minced garlic, mustard seeds, black peppercorns, and the bay leaf. Bring the mixture to a boil, stirring until the sugar and salt dissolve.

Pack the Jars:

Place the sliced yuca into clean, sterilized glass jars.

Pour the Brine:

Carefully pour the hot brine over the yuca in the jars, ensuring that the yuca is completely covered.

Seal the Jars:

Seal the jars with airtight lids.

Cool and Refrigerate:

Allow the jars to cool to room temperature before transferring them to the refrigerator.

The yuca pickles will be ready to eat in a few days and will continue to develop flavor over time.

Yuca Jam

Ingredients:

- 2 cups peeled and diced yuca
- 1 cup sugar
- Juice and zest of 1 lemon
- 1/2 cup water

Instructions:

Prepare the Yuca:

Peel and dice the yuca into small pieces.

Cook the Yuca:

- In a saucepan, combine the diced yuca, sugar, lemon juice, lemon zest, and water.
- Bring the mixture to a boil, then reduce the heat and simmer for about 20-25 minutes, or until the yuca is soft and can be easily mashed with a fork.

Mash and Cook:

- Mash the cooked yuca mixture with a fork or potato masher until it reaches your desired jam-like consistency.
- Continue to cook for an additional 5-10 minutes, stirring occasionally, until the jam thickens.

Cool and Store:

- Allow the yuca jam to cool before transferring it to clean, sterilized glass jars.
- Seal the jars with airtight lids.
- Store the yuca jam in the refrigerator.

Freeze-Drying Yuca
Instructions:
Prepare the Yuca:
Peel and slice the yuca into thin rounds or strips.
Blanch the Yuca:

- Bring a large pot of water to a boil and add a pinch of salt.
- Blanch the yuca slices in the boiling water for 3-4 minutes, then immediately transfer them to an ice bath to stop the cooking process.

Arrange on Trays:
Arrange the blanched yuca slices in a single layer on freeze-drying trays. Ensure they are not touching each other.
Freeze-Dry:

- Follow the manufacturer's instructions for your freeze-dryer. Typically, this involves freezing the yuca slices and then gradually reducing the pressure to remove moisture.
- This process can take several hours to a day, depending on your equipment.

Store:

- Once the freeze-drying process is complete, pack the freeze-dried yuca in airtight containers or vacuum-sealed bags.
- Store the freeze-dried yuca in a cool, dry place for long-term preservation.

Preserving yuca through pickling, jam-making, or freeze-drying allows you to enjoy this versatile root vegetable even when it's out of season. Whether you're creating tangy yuca pickles, sweet yuca jam, or freeze-drying yuca for future use, these preservation methods extend the shelf life of this culinary gem.

Chapter 15: Yuca in Dessert Fusion

Yuca, with its unique texture and subtle flavor, can be a surprising and delightful addition to dessert fusion creations. In this chapter, we'll explore how to incorporate yuca into three delicious and unexpected desserts: Yuca Tiramisu, Yuca and Matcha Ice Cream, and Yuca Cheesecake.

Yuca Tiramisu

Ingredients:

- 1 cup peeled and grated yuca
- 1 cup brewed strong coffee, cooled
- 3 tablespoons coffee liqueur (optional)
- 1 cup mascarpone cheese
- 1/2 cup powdered sugar
- 1 teaspoon vanilla extract
- 24-30 ladyfinger cookies
- Unsweetened cocoa powder for dusting
- Dark chocolate shavings for garnish (optional)

Instructions:

Prepare the Yuca Mixture:

In a mixing bowl, combine grated yuca, brewed coffee, and coffee liqueur (if using). Mix well and set aside to soak for about 10 minutes.

Prepare the Mascarpone Filling:

In a separate bowl, whisk together mascarpone cheese, powdered sugar, and vanilla extract until smooth and creamy.

Layer the Tiramisu:

Dip each ladyfinger cookie briefly into the yuca coffee mixture and arrange them in the bottom of a serving dish.

Add Yuca Layer:

Spread half of the yuca mixture over the ladyfingers.

Add Mascarpone Layer:

Layer half of the mascarpone filling on top of the yuca mixture.

Repeat:

Repeat the layers with the remaining ladyfingers, yuca mixture, and mascarpone filling.

Chill:

Cover the tiramisu and refrigerate for at least 4 hours or overnight to allow the flavors to meld.

Serve:

Before serving, dust the top with unsweetened cocoa powder and garnish with dark chocolate shavings if desired.

Yuca and Matcha Ice Cream

Ingredients:

- 2 cups peeled and cubed yuca
- 1 can (14 ounces) coconut milk
- 1/2 cup sugar
- 1 tablespoon matcha green tea powder
- 1 teaspoon vanilla extract
- Pinch of salt

Instructions:

Prepare the Yuca:

Peel and cube the yuca.

Cook the Yuca:

Boil or steam the yuca cubes until they are fork-tender, about 20-25 minutes. Drain and let them cool.

Blend the Ingredients:

In a blender, combine the cooked yuca, coconut milk, sugar, matcha green tea powder, vanilla extract, and a pinch of salt. Blend until smooth.

Churn the Ice Cream:

Pour the mixture into an ice cream maker and churn according to the manufacturer's instructions.

Freeze:

Transfer the churned ice cream to an airtight container and freeze for a few hours or until it reaches your desired ice cream consistency.

Serve:

Scoop and serve the yuca and matcha ice cream. It's a unique fusion of flavors and textures.

Yuca Cheesecake
Ingredients:

- 2 cups peeled and grated yuca
- 1 cup graham cracker crumbs
- 1/4 cup unsalted butter, melted
- 2 cups cream cheese
- 1 cup sugar
- 3 large eggs
- 1 teaspoon vanilla extract
- Zest and juice of 1 lemon
- Pinch of salt

Instructions:

Prepare the Crust:

In a mixing bowl, combine graham cracker crumbs and melted butter. Press the mixture into the bottom of a greased 9-inch springform pan to create the crust.

Prepare the Yuca Layer:

In another bowl, mix grated yuca with a pinch of salt. Spread this yuca layer over the graham cracker crust.

Prepare the Cheesecake Filling:

- In a separate bowl, beat cream cheese and sugar until smooth. Add eggs one at a time, beating well after each addition.
- Stir in vanilla extract, lemon zest, and lemon juice

Layer the Cheesecake:

Pour the cream cheese mixture over the yuca layer in the pan.

Bake:

Preheat your oven to 325°F (160°C). Bake the cheesecake for 45-50 minutes, or until the edges are set, and the center is slightly jiggly.

Cool and Chill:

Allow the cheesecake to cool to room temperature, then refrigerate for several hours or overnight.

Serve:

Slice and serve the yuca cheesecake, garnished with additional lemon zest if desired.

These dessert fusion recipes bring together the unique qualities of yuca with other delightful flavors to create memorable desserts. Whether you're indulging in the rich and creamy Yuca Tiramisu, savoring the earthy and vibrant Yuca and Matcha Ice Cream, or enjoying the sweet and tangy Yuca Cheesecake, these desserts offer a fusion of tastes and textures that will satisfy your sweet tooth.

Chapter 16: Health Benefits of Yuca

Yuca, also known as cassava, is not only a versatile and delicious root vegetable but also offers a range of health benefits. In this chapter, we'll explore the nutritional profile of yuca, its dietary advantages, and how to incorporate it into a healthy lifestyle through cooking.

Nutritional Profile

Yuca is a nutritious tuber with the following key nutrients:

- Carbohydrates: Yuca is a rich source of carbohydrates, making it an excellent energy source.
- Dietary Fiber: It contains dietary fiber, which aids in digestion and helps maintain digestive health.
- Vitamins: Yuca provides vitamins such as vitamin C, vitamin B6, and folate, which are essential for various bodily functions.
- Minerals: It is a good source of minerals like potassium, magnesium, and manganese.
- Antioxidants: Yuca contains antioxidants that help protect cells from oxidative damage.
- Resistant Starch: Some yuca varieties have resistant starch, a type of fiber that may have various health benefits, including improved blood sugar control and gut health.

Dietary Advantages

1. Gluten-Free Alternative:

Yuca flour (cassava flour) is naturally gluten-free, making it a safe option for individuals with celiac disease or gluten sensitivity.

2. Low in Fat:

Yuca is naturally low in fat, making it a heart-healthy choice.

3. High in Carbohydrates:

Yuca provides a substantial source of carbohydrates, which can help replenish energy levels.

4. Rich in Fiber:

The dietary fiber in yuca supports digestive health and may help prevent constipation.

5. Vitamins and Minerals:

Yuca offers essential vitamins and minerals, contributing to overall health and well-being.

6. Antioxidant Properties:

Some antioxidants in yuca can help combat oxidative stress and inflammation in the body.

Cooking for a Healthy Lifestyle

1. Steamed Yuca:

Steam yuca to preserve its nutrients and natural flavors. Serve it as a side dish with lean proteins and vegetables.

2. Yuca Fries:

Bake yuca fries instead of deep-frying for a healthier alternative to traditional French fries. Season them with herbs and spices for added flavor.

3. Yuca Mash:

Create a creamy yuca mash by boiling yuca until tender and mashing it with a touch of olive oil and herbs. Use it as a nutritious substitute for mashed potatoes.

4. Yuca in Salads:

Add boiled or steamed yuca cubes to salads for a boost of carbohydrates and fiber.

5. Yuca Soups:

Incorporate yuca into soups and stews to enhance their nutritional value and provide a hearty texture.

6. Gluten-Free Baking:

Use yuca flour in gluten-free baking recipes, such as pancakes, muffins, and bread, to create tasty treats for those with gluten sensitivities.

7. Balanced Meals:

Combine yuca with lean proteins, vegetables, and healthy fats to create balanced and nutritious meals.

Incorporating yuca into your diet can be a flavorful and nutritious choice. Whether you're looking for gluten-free options, heart-healthy carbohydrates, or a source of essential vitamins and minerals, yuca can play a valuable role in supporting your overall well-being.

Chapter 17: Yuca in Special Diets

Yuca, a versatile root vegetable, can be incorporated into various special diets with some adjustments and considerations. In this chapter, we'll explore how to include yuca in the ketogenic (keto) diet, the paleo diet, and low-carb diets while maintaining dietary compliance.

Yuca and Keto Diet

The keto diet is a high-fat, low-carbohydrate eating plan designed to encourage the body to enter a state of ketosis, where it primarily burns fat for energy. Yuca is relatively high in carbohydrates, which may pose challenges for keto followers. However, with moderation and mindful choices, you can still enjoy yuca in keto-friendly ways:

Portion Control: Limit the amount of yuca you consume in a keto meal. Smaller portions can help you manage your carbohydrate intake.

Balance with Fats: Pair yuca with keto-friendly fats like olive oil, coconut oil, or avocado to balance the macronutrient profile of your meal.

Fiber-Rich Foods: Include fiber-rich vegetables like leafy greens alongside yuca to increase satiety and minimize the impact on blood sugar.

Consider Resistant Starch: Some yuca varieties contain resistant starch, which may have a lower impact on blood sugar. Opt for varieties with higher resistant starch content when available.

Plan Meals Carefully: Plan your meals to ensure that your daily carbohydrate allowance is not exceeded. This may require tracking your yuca intake.

Keto-Friendly Recipes: Explore keto recipes that incorporate yuca as a small component in dishes that are primarily keto-friendly.

Yuca and Paleo Diet

The paleo diet focuses on foods that our ancestors might have consumed during the Paleolithic era, emphasizing whole, unprocessed foods. While yuca wasn't typically part of Paleolithic diets due to regional differences, it can still be enjoyed in moderation within the paleo framework:

Use Whole Yuca: opt for whole, unprocessed yuca over yuca products like flour or starch. Peel and cook yuca as you would any other root vegetable.

Incorporate Sparingly: Consume yuca in moderate amounts as an occasional starchy side dish or as part of a paleo-inspired meal.

Balance with Protein and Vegetables: Pair yuca with lean protein sources and plenty of vegetables to create balanced paleo-friendly meals.

Choose Nutrient-Dense Foods: Focus on nutrient-dense foods like lean meats, fish, vegetables, and healthy fats as the foundation of your paleo diet.

Variety is Key: Don't rely heavily on yuca. The key to paleo success is a diverse diet that includes a wide range of whole foods.

Avoid Processed Yuca Products: Stay away from processed yuca products like yuca chips or packaged snacks, as these may contain additives or unhealthy oils.

Yuca in Low-Carb Diets

Low-carb diets restrict carbohydrate intake to varying degrees. While yuca is relatively high in carbs, it can still be enjoyed in low-carb diets when consumed mindfully:

Portion Control: Consume yuca in moderation to stay within your daily carb limits.

Preparation Matters: Choose cooking methods that minimize carb content. Boiling or steaming yuca can help reduce its glycemic load.

Balanced Meals: Pair yuca with protein, healthy fats, and low-carb vegetables to create balanced low-carb meals.

Track Carbs: If you follow a strict low-carb diet, keep track of your daily carbohydrate intake to ensure you don't exceed your carb limit.

Consider Resistant Starch: Some yuca varieties contain resistant starch, which may have a lower impact on blood sugar. Look for these varieties if available.

Explore Low-Carb Recipes: Seek out low-carb recipes that incorporate yuca in a way that aligns with your dietary goals.

Remember that individual carb tolerance varies, so it's essential to tailor your yuca consumption to your specific dietary needs and goals when following special diets.

Chapter 18: Culinary Adventures with Yuca

Yuca, with its versatile nature and rich history, invites culinary adventurers to explore a world of flavors and possibilities. In this chapter, we'll embark on exciting culinary adventures with yuca, from discovering it on food tours to exploring sustainable yuca farming practices and delving into fusion cuisine.

Yuca in Food Tours

Discovering Yuca Around the World

Yuca is a global treasure, and food tours can be a delightful way to explore its various preparations and cultural significance. Here are some destinations where you can savor yuca in different forms:

Colombia: Explore Colombian cuisine on a food tour to discover yuca dishes like arepas de yuca and sancocho.

Cuba: Visit local markets and street vendors in Cuba to try yuca con mojo and yuca frita.

Africa: Travel to West African countries like Ghana and Nigeria to experience yuca-based dishes like fufu and cassava leaf soup.

Brazil: Enjoy Brazilian snacks like coxinhas, which often contain yuca flour, or try yuca-based sweets like pão de queijo.

Caribbean Islands: Discover yuca-based dishes like yuca con bacalao in the Caribbean islands.

Southeast Asia: Explore yuca's presence in Southeast Asian cuisines, particularly in dishes from the Philippines and Thailand.

Cooking Workshops and Culinary Experiences

Consider joining cooking workshops or culinary experiences during your food tour destinations. Learn how to prepare yuca dishes from local chefs and gain hands-on experience with this versatile ingredient.

Yuca Farming and Sustainability

Sustainable Yuca Farming Practices

Yuca is a staple crop in many regions, and sustainable farming practices are essential to ensure its availability and reduce its environmental impact. Sustainable farming methods for yuca include:

Crop Rotation: Implement crop rotation to maintain soil fertility and prevent soil depletion.

Conservation Tillage: Adopt no-till or reduced-till practices to reduce soil erosion and conserve moisture.

Biodiversity: Promote biodiversity on yuca farms by intercropping with other crops and planting cover crops.

Organic Farming: Consider organic farming methods to reduce the use of synthetic pesticides and fertilizers.

Water Management: Implement efficient irrigation techniques to conserve water resources.

Community-Based Farming Initiatives

Support community-based yuca farming initiatives that prioritize sustainable practices and empower local communities. These initiatives often contribute to economic development and food security in rural areas.

Yuca in Fusion Cuisine

Exploring Fusion Flavors

Fusion cuisine combines elements from different culinary traditions to create exciting and innovative dishes. Here are some fusion ideas to infuse yuca into global flavors:

Asian Fusion: Create yuca dumplings with Asian-inspired fillings or incorporate yuca noodles into stir-fries.

Mediterranean Fusion: Make yuca-based flatbreads and serve them with Mediterranean toppings like hummus and tzatziki.

Latin Fusion: Experiment with yuca in Latin-inspired dishes like yuca empanadas with unique fillings or yuca tacos with Latin flavors.

African Fusion: Prepare yuca-based stews and soups infused with West African spices and flavors.

Tropical Fusion: Blend yuca into tropical smoothies or desserts, combining it with fruits like mango and coconut.

Inventive Yuca Desserts

Explore the sweeter side of yuca in fusion desserts. Try creating yuca-based sweets like yuca and coconut cake with tropical fruit compote or yuca and chocolate brownies with a hint of spice.

Culinary adventures with yuca offer a unique opportunity to explore diverse cuisines, sustainable farming practices, and the creative world of fusion cuisine.

Chapter 19: Cooking Tips and Tricks

Cooking with yuca can be a delightful experience, and having a few tips and tricks up your sleeve can make your culinary adventures even more successful. In this chapter, we'll explore tips for yuca substitutions, troubleshooting common issues with yuca dishes, and creative ways to garnish your dishes with yuca.

Yuca Substitutions

When You're Out of Yuca

Potatoes: In many recipes, you can substitute yuca with potatoes. While the flavors are different, the textures can be quite similar when prepared in the same way.

Sweet Potatoes: For a slightly sweeter twist, consider using sweet potatoes as a yuca substitute.

Plantains: In some Latin dishes, ripe plantains can be used as a substitute for yuca. They offer a similar starchy texture.

Parsnips: In recipes where the earthy flavor of yuca is not crucial, parsnips can provide a similar texture and a mild, nutty taste.

Taro Root: Taro root can be a suitable substitute for yuca in Asian and tropical dishes, offering a starchy texture.

Cassava Flour: If you're looking for a yuca flour substitute in gluten-free recipes, consider using other gluten-free flours like almond flour or coconut flour.

Arrowroot Flour: For thickening sauces or soups, arrowroot flour can replace yuca starch.

Remember that substitutions may slightly alter the flavor and texture of your dish, so it's a good idea to adjust seasonings and cooking times accordingly.

Troubleshooting Yuca Dishes

Common Issues and Solutions

Yuca is Tough or Stringy: Overcooking can make yuca tough or stringy. Ensure you cook it until it's tender but not mushy. If it's still stringy, you can remove the fibrous core before cooking.

Yuca is Gummy or Sticky: Overcooked yuca can become gummy. To avoid this, test the doneness by inserting a fork or knife; it should go in easily. If it's gummy, try cooking for a shorter time.

Yuca is Bland: Yuca's natural flavor can be mild, so don't be afraid to season it generously with salt, spices, herbs, or sauces to enhance its taste.

Yuca is Hard to Peel: Peeling yuca can be challenging due to its tough outer layer. Use a sharp knife, cut it into manageable sections, and remove the waxy skin carefully.

Yuca is Too Dry: If your yuca dish turns out too dry, consider adding a bit of liquid (such as broth or olive oil) and gently reheating it.

Garnishing with Yuca

Creative Ways to Showcase Yuca

Yuca Chips: Thinly slice yuca, deep-fry or bake the slices until crisp, and use them as a garnish for salads, soups, or casseroles.

Yuca Crisps: Create yuca crisps by frying yuca slices until golden and seasoning them with your favorite spices. These make a crunchy topping for dishes.

Yuca Curls: Spiralize yuca to make beautiful yuca curls. Use them as an artistic garnish for main courses or desserts.

Yuca Puree Swirls: Make a silky yuca puree and use it to create decorative swirls on plates, adding an elegant touch to your dishes.

Yuca Cubes: Cube cooked yuca and skewer them with colorful vegetables for a visually appealing kabob garnish.

Yuca Flowers: Carve yuca slices into intricate flower shapes and use them as a striking garnish for special occasions.

Garnishing with yuca not only adds visual appeal to your dishes but also showcases the versatility of this root vegetable. Get creative and experiment with different shapes and presentations to elevate your culinary creations.

Yuca Around the World

As we come to the end of our culinary journey with yuca, it's evident that this versatile root vegetable has made its mark on kitchens and cultures worldwide. In this concluding chapter, we reflect on yuca's global presence and ponder its future in cuisine.

Yuca's Global Presence

Yuca, also known as cassava, has transcended borders and found its place in cuisines across the globe. From Latin America to Africa, Asia to the Caribbean, and beyond, yuca has woven itself into the fabric of diverse culinary traditions.

Latin America: In Latin American countries like Colombia, Venezuela, and Cuba, yuca is celebrated in dishes like arepas de yuca, yuca con mojo, and sancocho. Its presence in Latin cuisine is undeniable.

Africa: Yuca's journey from South America to Africa during the colonial era resulted in the integration of this root vegetable into African cuisines. Dishes like fufu and cassava leaf soup showcase its African influence.

Southeast Asia: In Southeast Asia, particularly in the Philippines and Thailand, yuca is used in various savory and sweet dishes, showcasing its adaptability in different culinary contexts.

Caribbean Islands: The Caribbean islands boast a rich culinary tradition where yuca is a staple. From yuca con bacalao to yuca fries, it adds depth and flavor to Caribbean cuisine.

Global Fusion: Yuca has also found its way into fusion cuisine, where chefs combine elements from different culinary traditions to create exciting and innovative dishes. Its versatility shines in these fusion creations.

The Future of Yuca in Cuisine

As we look ahead, the future of yuca in cuisine appears promising. Its versatility, nutritional value, and adaptability to various dietary preferences position it as a dynamic ingredient that will continue to inspire chefs and home cooks alike.

Innovation: Chefs and culinary innovators will likely continue to experiment with yuca, creating new dishes that fuse global flavors and showcase its unique qualities.

Healthy Eating: Yuca's role in gluten-free, paleo, and low-carb diets will likely grow as more people seek alternative ingredients that align with their dietary choices.

Sustainability: Sustainable yuca farming practices will gain importance as awareness of environmental issues increases. Supporting sustainable yuca farming initiatives can contribute to a more eco-conscious culinary world.

Global Cuisine: As our world becomes more interconnected, access to diverse ingredients like yuca will increase, leading to greater integration of global flavors into everyday cooking.

Food Tours: Culinary enthusiasts will continue to embark on food tours to explore yuca in its various forms and cultural contexts, fostering appreciation for this remarkable root vegetable.

Yuca's journey from its origins in South America to becoming a cherished ingredient in kitchens around the world is a testament to the power of food to transcend boundaries and bring people together. As we savor its flavors, let us celebrate the rich tapestry of culinary traditions that yuca has woven into, and eagerly anticipate the delicious innovations and discoveries that the future holds.

Thank you for joining us on this flavorful adventure with yuca, and may your culinary explorations continue to be as diverse and delightful as the world of yuca cuisine.